Judith Samson & Denis Maryk

G000149369

FAMILY LIBRARY
of
WORLD TRAVEL

The Temple of Heaven, Peking
previous page. This is the most perfect temple in China. Located in an extensive walled park, its unusual shape, color and setting give an impression of great splendor, but also of peace. With its brilliant blue-glazed roof tiles representing heaven, the temple was built entirely of wood and without the use of a single nail, for emperors of the Ming dynasty. To the south is a smaller, simpler temple, called the Imperial Vault of Heaven, whose most striking feature is a circular wall surrounding an outer courtyard which has a loud echo. To one side is a triple-tiered white marble altar where the Emperor used to come each year to pray for a good harvest, amid clouds of incense and to the sound of tinkling bells.

Japanese lady with paper umbrella.
The grace and dignity of the Japanese woman is legendary. Here we see the traditional silk kimono with the large sleeves sweeping down to emphasize the sleek design of the garment. The more heavily embroidered kimonos are usually worn by brides, young girls or geisha. There are several ways to wear the kimono, and various lengths and styles are suitable for different occasions. For example, the very long sleeves are worn for a formal function. The Japanese umbrella, called *bangasa*, is made of oiled paper and bamboo and will be remarkably resilient to even the heaviest downpour. The curved Japanese bridge has been the subject of many fine woodcuts of the 19th century.

First published in 1985
for AGT Publishing
by Octopus Books Limited
59 Grosvenor Street
London W1, England

© 1985 Octopus Books Limited

ISBN 0-933521-18-9

Produced by Mandarin Publishers Ltd
22a Westlands Road
Quarry Bay, Hong Kong

Jacket Photography: Zefa Picture Library

CONTENTS

INTRODUCTION

Seven hundred years after the West first made contact with the Far East, this strange, exotic and mysterious corner of the world still contrasts sharply with the way of life and attitudes of the West. This is primarily because the people of the East live very close to their gods, and because the spiritual side of life is as natural and real to them as the temporal. It is this overflowing of the spiritual into all areas of living that gives the East the depth and richness for which it is justly famous.

Against this background, the East has embraced many aspects of Western culture. This has been achieved with such amazing speed and vigor that at times the world has looked on in astonishment. But the traditional way of life is still in evidence, which makes traveling through the Orient like being in a time machine. The English-speaking traveler will not have many language problems journeying through Hong Kong or Singapore, as the years of colonial rule have left a strong linguistic tradition. But this can lead the unwary to believe that a common tongue indicates a common culture. It does not.

Each of the countries of the Orient has its own distinguishing features which will leave visitors with a strong impression of variety and contrast. Hong Kong, with its mainly Chinese population, is a vast trading center for the East, and has only superficially disguised its Chinese culture beneath the hustle and bustle of worldwide commercial activity. Singapore has several ethnic groups – Chinese, Malays and Indians – which are quite rigidly defined, and which manage to maintain their separate identities by keeping their own festivals and traditions. Thailand has been subjected to comparatively little Western influence. It remains unaffected, particularly in the rural parts where farmers carry on planting and harvesting in much the same way as their ancestors did. The landscape, from tropical rain forests to wooded mountains, is largely unspoiled. In China, which has the largest population in the world, the people display a strong national pride and a sense of collectivism rather than individualism. However, the uniformity of the Chinese dress belies the fact that there are many different peoples within the Chinese socialist framework. Finally, the Japanese are world leaders in many areas of modern technology and, while they sometimes rush around at superspeed, they also spend hours in contemplation of the apparent simplicity of the Japanese tea ceremony.

Variety, then, is the essence of the new Far East, where people have ingeniously incorporated aspects of Western living into their distinctly Oriental way of life. Wherever you travel in the Orient your senses will be bombarded by different sights, sounds and smells which are sure to leave you with a vivid impression of exotic mystery and exciting contrasts.

The city by night. This is one of the world's most magnificent and unforgettable views – Hong Kong harbor from the island's highest hill, the tree-covered Victoria Peak. In the foreground are tall, illuminated skyscraper blocks; beyond is the curve of the harbor, bustling with boats; and in the shadowy background are the gently rising hills of Kowloon. The best way up to the Peak is by tram, a funicular railway which zooms up the steep hillside to a height of 1800 feet above sea level in barely eight minutes. At the top, there is a restaurant.

Hong Kong skyline. With their high, flat sterns, junks are not very seaworthy, but are ideal for carrying freight within the harbor, and they have plenty of room for the families who live on them. As they sail gracefully and silently past the immensely tall concrete skyscrapers which line the waterfront, the visitor can imagine, in contrast, the scenery of a century ago, when the hillsides were covered with dense vegetation.

HONG KONG

Hong Kong Island · Kowloon · The New Territories

A thriving, capitalist colony on the southern tip of communist China, Hong Kong is one of the most fascinating places in the Far East. It is a colony of contrasts: almost all the population is Chinese, but there are strong British overtones; it is home for both millionaire property tycoons and simple peasants; it is a guardian of age-old Chinese customs and an innovator of new technology. These varied ingredients seem to lend it extra verve and energy.

For visitors, the most glittering attraction is the treasure-filled shops – laden with wondrous goods from East and West – which never seem to close. Hong Kong visibly throbs with life 24 hours a day. Its bright and bustling streets are so crowded that people seem to spill off the pavements, and even the new high-level walkways and underpasses can barely cope. But beneath the glare and glamor beats a truly Chinese heart. The people are very hard-working and enterprising, and they warmly welcome Western visitors.

Exciting and exhilarating, Hong Kong is one of the economic miracles of the modern world. It has successfully blended Eastern business acumen and hard work with Western technology, to become one of the most admired commercial centers.

When the colony came under British rule over 140 years ago, the then Prime Minister called it a 'barren rock'. Today, he would hardly recognize it. The lower part of the north side of the rock of Hong Kong Island is covered with serried ranks of glass and concrete skyscrapers, some over 50 stories high. More are being built, and their construction continues through the night under glaring floodlights. But the island is very pretty, with gentle hills and pretty bays, and splendid views from Victoria Peak down to Hong Kong harbor and the sea. The roads curve round the hillsides, in places like a switchback system, until they finally descend to one of the many bays.

Hong Kong is the international business hub, but only one part of the colony. The second part is Kowloon, across the harbor, on the very tip of the Chinese mainland. Many visitors find the ferry crossing one of the most memorable parts of their trip. The green and white Star Ferry service efficiently carries hundreds of thousands of passengers across the harbor every day. As the ferry draws away to the repeated clanging of the ship's bell, you are taken into the harbor which is full of sampans,

Typical shopping street. Hong Kong is often called the world's biggest bazaar, and scenes like this explain why. The streets vibrate with color and noise and spicy smells, and every visitor becomes engulfed in the excitement. The signs, many indecipherable to the Westerner, are advertisements, but their impact is the same whether or not they are fully understood. Often loud music blares forth and, together with the rattle of the old trams and the roar of modern vehicles, adds another element to the bombardment of your senses. With so much traffic it is not surprising that many a tourist is tempted to buy whatever he stumbles upon first, rather than struggle through the crowds to the next shop in the hope of a better price.

Man Mo Temple *right.* This is the oldest Buddhist temple in Hong Kong, thought to have been built in 1848. Situated amongst the antique shops of Hollywood Road, on a busy part of the island, this temple has always been very popular. The visitor can peer through the ever-open doors and be almost stifled by the heavy pall of smoke caused by the great coils of incense hanging from the ceiling, and by the burning of joss sticks. The two most important gods here are Man, the scholar god, and Mo, the soldier god. On important festivals, like Chinese New Year, the gods are carried around the streets in gold-plated sedan chairs which are kept in the Temple.

Traveling in comfort *below.* This method of carrying babies is practical, convenient and costs nothing. The baby is securely attached and the operation of hoisting him onto the shoulders is carried out deftly. Chinese mothers have always carried their babies in this way; in a crowded environment like Hong Kong, there would be little room to push a baby carriage. The babies themselves seem to find this mode of transport very soothing and generally sleep throughout their journey.

tankers, small motorboats, and other ferries busily hooting and belching out steam. It is possible now to travel between Hong Kong Island and Kowloon by road through the underpass or by underground train, but you would miss the view of the island waterfront: the gigantic multi-story tower blocks are dwarfed by the green hills behind. While you are still looking back there is a jolt as the rubber tires on the ferry hit the landing stage. You are in Kowloon, famous for its ever-open shops, luxurious hotels and exotic nightlife.

The third area of Hong Kong, and by far the largest, is called The New Territories. It is a rural area, but increasingly it is being used for housing. The contrast to the Kowloon way of life is fascinating. Duck and fish farms stretch into the distance until they reach and merge with similar farms in China. You can go to Lok Ma Chau, on the Chinese border, by train or by road, and look across the river Shun Chun into China. The Chinese countryside offers similar scenery of gentle hills, and paddy fields being tended by crouching peasants planting rice in the shallow water, or farmers slowly leading water buffalo through the mud. All this is a far cry from most visitors' impression of Hong Kong. But it is just as real.

Back on the island, the color and bustle is invigorating. Just wandering through the streets you can see young girls in the latest Western fashions, elderly Chinese *amahs* (servants) wearing shapeless dark jackets and trousers, and even the native women from the Hakka tribe, wearing their characteristic flat straw hats that have a hole through the crown and a short black curtain hanging round the brim.

Choosing a bird *left*. There is a wonderful variety of goods on offer in Hong Kong's shops. By far the most interesting are the open-fronted shops and the street trading stalls used·by the Chinese. Caged birds are popular with the Chinese, not only because they take up little space, but because the people love the sound of birdsong.

Tiger Balm Gardens *below*. High above Causeway Bay, sheltered by the sub-tropical vegetation, are the renowned Tiger Balm Gardens. There are no tigers here; the Gardens are named after a very successful ointment that the maker's claimed could cure a wide variety of ills, from toothache to scorpion bites. The entrepreneurs who produced Tiger Balm (brothers called Aw Boon Hawr and Aw Boon Par), became millionaires, and provided these Gardens. They are bright and gaudy, with pagodas and statues (from Mickey Mouse to Buddhist gods) and pools and grottoes. Winding paths and flights of steps lead from one section to another. Children particularly love the Gardens which, although often crowded, are always great fun.

The boat people *below*. There is a constant housing shortage in Hong Kong – today's population is double that of 10 years ago. To overcome this desperate situation, thousands of families choose to live on boats. Some people never live on dry land. It is a colorful scene – children and dogs, chickens and washing all vying for space. Luckily, no one ever seems to fall overboard. This floating population mainly resides in Aberdeen Harbor, the island's oldest settlement.

Few visitors can resist the temptation of the galaxy of shops, and the hope of a bargain. There are air-conditioned multi-story shopping complexes (such as Ocean City in Kowloon) full of lavishly decorated boutiques, selling fashions and electronic goods, jewelry and cameras. There are conventional department stores, small family-run shops and, of course, outdoor street markets where it is normal to bargain. Hong Kong acts as an outlet for goods from China through special shops (such as China Products) which sell wonderful Oriental merchandise: intricately carved ivory and wood, fragile porcelain, pale cool jade and hand-embroidered linen. Today Chinese-made clothes are designed to suit Western tastes although the sizes may often favor small people. You don't have to be there very long to be able to have some clothes specially made – silk shirts can be made to order in three days.

Cheung Chau bun festival *right.*
Cheung Chau is only an hour's ferry ride from Hong Kong, but it remains a most rural island. Every year in April or May (depending on the lunar calendar) the islanders hold a four-day bun festival. They celebrate with religious ceremonies and noisy processions through the streets. Small children are beautifully made up in gorgeous silks. They are carried aloft on wires so that they appear to be floating. On the last day, buns are distributed to ensure good luck through the coming year.

The most interesting shops of all are those patronized by the Chinese, particularly food shops. You'll see hawkers skillfully peeling pineapples, and colorful, exotic fruits like mangoes or papayas displayed on stalls. Some specialties, like the hundred-year-old eggs, quite black and nestling in a barrel of peat, might leave you curious but untempted.

One of the delights of Hong Kong is the cooking, at which the Chinese excel. Their cuisine demands detailed attention to color, texture and presentation. The food is so fresh and flavoring so subtle, that it is often hard for the visitor to choose where and what to eat. The style of cooking of every region of China is represented in Hong Kong but the Cantonese style dominates since Canton is the region of China geographically closest to Hong Kong. The taste of Cantonese food is distinguished by the fresh ingredients which are cooked quickly, often stir-fried, and flavored with ginger or onion. At lunchtime, *dim sum* (small snacks) are very popular. They include mouthful-sized steamed dumplings, filled with the tastiest meat, fish or vegetables, and served in wooden-sided bamboo baskets. In Chinese restaurants, it is always better to be in a large group so that more dishes can be tried.

On Hong Kong Island is Ocean Park, a pleasure ground with one of the world's largest displays of ocean life. Many of the creatures, including dolphins, sealions and killer whales, perform daily in the

Floating restaurants *above*. Aberdeen's restaurants ensure that you have a fine view while you savor a delicious Cantonese meal. They are brightly lit in garish colors, and a full four stories high. You can go there for lunch or dinner, and the fish is usually recommended as it is caught from tanks behind the kitchen once you have made your choice. Garoupa, prawns (shrimp) and crab are almost always offered, but there's a mouth-watering menu of other delights.

Resting rickshaws *right*. In spite of being engineless, a rickshaw can often be a very fast means of transport through Hong Kong. The elderly drivers are very nimble and dart through the traffic jams. The place to hire rickshaws is at the Star Ferry terminal, but make sure you arrange a price before you set off. Rickshaw driving is a diminishing occupation as the present administration is not issuing any new licenses. The drivers are quite happy to be photographed while they wait for business, as long as you pay them for the privilege.

outdoor Ocean Theater and are thrilling to watch.

Hong Kong nightlife caters for all tastes. There are harbor tours which often include dinner at one of Aberdeen's floating restaurants, or you can go up to Victoria Peak and watch the lights of the city twinkling in the distance. After dinner there is still plenty to do. Bars and nightclubs, where you can drink and relax, are open until late.

TRAVEL TIPS

Take cotton clothes because the weather is quite humid throughout the year. The most pleasant months are from October to April, the stickiest are July and August. May to September are the wettest months, so take an umbrella or buy a Chinese oiled paper one while you are there. Typhoons occur in the late summer – there's plenty of notice, but observe the typhoon warnings if traveling at that time of year.

Hong Kong has many different types of public transport. Most are cheap and all are crowded, especially during the morning and evening rush hours and at weekends. On the ferries, the upper deck is first class. Tickets are issued only on the subway (Mass Transit Railway – MTR). On other vehicles you must drop the exact money for your fare into a box. There are change booths at the Star Ferry landing stages and at MTR stations.

Meals are eaten quite early. Lunch is from midday, and Chinese restaurants get very crowded. When you want another pot of tea, turn the teapot lid upside down. It is polite to try using chopsticks.

Always ask a Chinese person before taking his photograph – they are sometimes unwilling to be photographed.

Typhoon shelter, Yaumati *above*. The months the boat people dread most are July to September when the typhoons may strike. It is not just the heavy rain that they fear, but the fast swirling winds, which can reach 75 miles an hour, and will snatch up a boat and hurl it against another one, causing devastation on board. But nowadays, the cyclones can be spotted by modern meteorological equipment several hours before they hit, and there is usually enough warning for most people to shelter. This boatperson has reached the typhoon shelter – an L-shaped breakwater – well in time.

SINGAPORE

Chinatown • Serangoon Road

The Harbor. This is one of Singapore's most spectacular sights. As the crossroads between East and West, Singapore is now the second largest port in the world.

A diamond-shaped tropical island set in a turquoise sea, inhabited by warm and friendly people from many ethnic backgrounds...this is Singapore. It is a mixture of Oriental mysticism, Indian astuteness and Malayan modesty which have blended together to form a harmonious whole. While each group of native people preserves its ancient customs and exotic festivals, they have all responded to the demands of progress. The result is one of the most thriving cities of the Far East, whose prosperity is now firmly based on shopping and shipping.

Singapore became independent in 1965 after over 140 years of British rule. It is developing rapidly, through an extensive rebuilding program which aims to provide a better environment for its ever-growing population. The visitor will find it a fascinating kaleidoscope of life and color, where elements of the past merge with those of the present, and where food is treated with great reverence. Each person is aware of his own background, and lives and works in the hope of a continuing harmony in the future.

Singapore has all the necessary ingredients of a paradise island: warm weather, lovely beaches, lush vegetation and colorful birds and flowers. Lying just 100 miles north of the equator, Singapore has turned these natural features to her own advantage and the very clean, modern city, bristling with skyscrapers, smart hotels and shopping centers, is softened by the generous planting of shrubs and flowers, even over traffic islands and street lights. The streets themselves are planted with shady trees, transforming them into gracious boulevards

Yet only 150 years ago, this island was covered with dense forest and crocodile-filled mangrove swamps. The man who saw Singapore's potential as a trading port, a crossroads between East and West, was Sir Stamford Raffles, a British colonial administrator. He planned a new town and divided it up into separate areas for the different groups of people who were then living there – Chinese, Arabs and Hindus. They still preserve their own religions and festivals, cultural traditions, languages, cuisines and styles of dress.

Three-quarters of today's population are Chinese. It is a fascinating experience to wander into Chinatown and imbibe the atmosphere of the East in the crowded narrow alleys, festooned with washing hanging

Street temple. Fun and festivals are part of everyday life in Singapore. The Chinese festival of Hungry Ghosts falls in the seventh lunar month, when it is thought that the souls of the dead return to wander the earth. To appease and honor them the Chinese prepare food for them, and burn joss sticks and imitation paper money. In the streets, local stall-holders cooperate to build street temples and hold lavish celebrations, including Chinese opera, to entertain the spirits and ensure a prosperous year for themselves. Once the ghosts have departed, the living sit down to eat what is left. But, the Chinese say, the food is mysteriously tasteless.

19

Calligrapher at work *left*. Calligraphy is one of the most ancient of Chinese arts, and devotees will gaze for hours at a beautiful example. It requires infinite skill and patience, for a stroke that is of the wrong length or thickness can entirely alter the meaning of the word. Years of practice are needed but once he has become expert the calligrapher will always be in demand. The frequency of Chinese festivals means that he is constantly being asked to write slogans for decorative banners which are hung over doorways in homes, shops, offices and restaurants. What may be unintelligible squiggles to the Western eye, are messages of good luck to the Oriental eye.

Tiger Balm Gardens: the entrance *right*. These gardens were built by the same brothers who were responsible for those in Hong Kong (page 11). They are just as popular, particularly with the local people. The main gateway is reminiscent of entering a Chinese temple, with colored tiles in the upward curving roof. Inside, the gardens are a strange mixture of statues and grottoes and fairy scenes. They extend over an area of eight acres on a hillside on the west coast.

Tiger Balm Gardens: every figure tells a story *left*. The mixture of figures is surprising – Buddhas and mermaids, tigers and white rats. Several tableaux aim to give lessons on morality, and there are panels illustrating the seven deadly sins. The evil doers are crushed between stones, chopped in half or thrown into pots of boiling oil. The message is quite clear: reckless living will lead to poverty and crime. Less controversial figures are taken from Chinese folklore, and there is also an international corner with a Greek discus thrower in a fig leaf, hopping kangaroos and the Statue of Liberty. An unusual place to visit, but lots of fun.

Food stall: eating 'al fresco' *right*. The warm weather is very conducive to eating outside, and one of the most exciting Singapore experiences is to go to a food stall. These date from the time of Sir Stamford Raffles, though now the stalls may be set out in modern food centers as well as in back alleys. Using fairly basic equipment, these one-man kitchens produce, at great speed, some of the tastiest and cheapest dishes in town. The names of the dishes, and the prices, are displayed in English, and the visitor should first reserve a table for himself, then go round the different stalls and place his order. Regular visits from government inspectors ensure that a correct level of hygiene is maintained. In a frenzied, chaotic atmosphere all visitors eat a memorable meal.

from poles, and watch the craftsmen ply their ancient trades. Some skillfully cut paper into shapes of houses or cars, to be burnt at Chinese funerals, some fashion large candles for temple ceremonies, while others carve clogs, etch Chinese characters into stone or tell your fortune. The visitor will be surprised at the strange products on sale in the medicine shops – dried reptiles, flowers, roots and barks – which form the basis for many a potion. Green grass oil is said to relieve sprained muscles, flying fox soup will cure asthma and turtle soup is recommended for backache.

Close by, in and around Serangoon Road, is the predominantly Indian area, where tiny shops sell wares typical of Southern India – silk saris, glittering jewelry, clay cooking pots – and, of course, rice. Fat sacks of beans and lentils, tin trays of nuts and spices, and mounds of brightly colored vegetables and fruit might persuade the visitor that he is in India. The all-pervading aroma of this area is exotic: incense and spices mix with the sweet fragrance of jasmine. While the Indian ladies wear fine silk saris and jingling bangles, less prosperous traders squat on the pavement trying to eke a living from the sale of betel nuts or garlands of scented flowers.

One of the smallest ethnic pockets is the area where the Muslim traders sell their wares – mostly rattan and basketware piled in huge heaps, but also filigree jewelry and precious stones. Batik material is sold in a riot of colors and designs, for sarongs, tablecloths and as ready-made clothing. The market is close to Singapore's biggest mosque, the gold-domed Sultan Mosque, and nearby prayer rugs, holy books and pilgrim's garb are sold, for those who want to turn to Mecca and pray.

Away from this intoxicating ethnic area are modern shops catering for the tourist. Many are in multi-level air-conditioned complexes, and the dazzling displays of duty-free goods makes shopping both attractive and difficult. Best buys are watches, cameras and hi-fi equipment, but there are also bargains in carpets, jade, silk and antiques. It is usually possible to have tailor-made clothes completed within 24 hours. And while it is perfectly possible to find Western-style food, visitors should try the wide range of Eastern foods available – Chinese, Indian (north and south), Indonesian and Malay being the main ones.

Raffles Hotel *left.* Once the most famous hotel in the Far East, the Raffles Hotel is one of the last bastions of the island's colonial past. Named after the founding father of Singapore, the hotel is built in the French renaissance style. Its elegant interior has marble floors and lofty ceilings, with a magnificent balustraded staircase leading to the upper floors. In the early part of this century it was the social center for British administrators in Singapore and visiting dignitaries. British writers, such as Rudyard Kipling and Somerset Maugham, frequently stayed there, and described the hotel in their works. Set in a large garden and shaded by tall palm trees, the Raffles Hotel is a stately reminder of a more leisured age.

Crocodile farm *below.* The natural inhabitants of Singapore, before the arrival of man, were snakes and crocodiles, living around the mangrove swamps. Today, crocodiles are bred for their valuable skins, and visitors can see about 400 live specimens on a farm. They are kept in large pools, and visitors are strongly warned not to feed them.

Lion dancers seeing in the New Year
above. With its multi-racial
population, Singapore celebrates
more festivals than almost any other
country in the world. Visitors are
warmly welcomed to them all, and in
particular to the Chinese New Year,
which usually falls in February. This
is a family occasion more than a
public one, but the city celebrates
with the Chingay Parade. This is a
noisy procession which passes
through the streets – jugglers,
acrobats, stiltwalkers and
swordsmen brandish giant flags
which they skillfully manipulate. One
of the most attractive displays is the
colorful lion dance, where the
performers twist and turn to the
beating of cymbals and drums.

As well as their own individual cuisines, Singapore's different groups
fervently follow their own faiths. You will see domed mosques with
delicate minarets, traditional Chinese temples with colorful roofs,
temples containing great statues of Buddha and, perhaps the most
ornate temples of all, those of the Hindu faith. The oldest on the island
is the Sri Mariamman, with a flamboyantly decorated tower encrusted
with gaudily painted statues of gods in human form. Hand in hand with
faith, go the festivals. Hardly a month goes by without one, and by far
the most spectacular is the Hindu festival of Thaipusam. Male devotees
ask forgiveness and throw themselves into a trance, then pierce their
bodies, including their tongues, with skewers, to form a large steel
cage, on which are hung fruit and feathers. The penitents stagger
through the streets on nail-studded sandals until they reach the Chettiar
Temple where they collapse in a religious spasm. Miraculously, when
the skewers are removed, no blood is spilt.

Away from the hubbub of the city, there are tropical oases of peace
and greenery. The native orchid thrives, and in parks, gardens and
nature reserves the observant visitor will spot this normally shy and
delicate plant in a variety of colors and sizes. In the Bukit Timah
Reserve, the original lush vegetation has been preserved, and trails take
you past dense ferns, creepers and massive trees. Across the sea are
Singapore's islands, many of which are blissfully pristine while others
have been developed for tourists. The most popular is Sentosa which
can be reached by cable-car. It has fortress museums, coral displays
and endless sandy beaches.

The best way of spending an evening, is to take in the varied nightlife,
for the streets become even livelier and more entertaining after dusk.
You might be lucky enough to come across a noisy Chinese street
opera, called a *wayang*, accompanied by crashing gongs and cymbals.

Malayan girl *below*. Singapore was just a Malay fishing village when Sir Stamford Raffles arrived in the early part of the last century, but soon traders from neighboring islands settled there too. During the last hundred years, the Malays have watched large numbers of Indians and Chinese come to the island of Singapore and set up prosperous businesses. The Malay people are not by nature dynamic traders, and today they total only about 15% of the population. Gentle and friendly, they work mainly in government offices and in the police force. Religion and the family are the dominating influences in their lives; they are followers of the Muslim faith. The wail of the muezzin can regularly be heard from the towering minarets of the golden-domed Sultan Mosque.

One thing is certain, a few days in Singapore will be unforgettable, and the sooner you go there the better.

TRAVEL TIPS

As the weather is always warm and humid, cotton clothes are best. Short, sharp showers fall most of the year, but are heaviest during the November to January monsoon, so take an umbrella. Be careful when stepping off the curb as there are deep gulleys to drain off excess rainwater.

When entering a mosque, temple or even a private home, it is customary to remove your shoes. When invited to someone's house, it is polite to take a small gift, such as fruit. Knives and forks are not always used, so try to get the hang of eating any Chinese meal with chopsticks. It is easier, and customary, to eat an Indian meal with your fingers.

Singapore's reputation as a clean and tidy city has been earned through the imposition of strict penalties rather than from natural civic-mindedness. Visitors are not immune to these penalties, and can be fined for dropping litter, jaywalking and smoking in public places. One legacy of British rule is that traffic keeps to the left, and to reduce the number of vehicles going into the town center each day, drivers have to buy a daily license to enter the Central Business District.

Finally, men with long hair are not welcome and may be invited into the barber's shop at their point of immigration.

Instant Asia show *right*. Total immersion into Singapore's culture is the aim of this daily performance for visitors. With their diverse background and rich traditions the Chinese, Indians and Malays each have a lot to offer in the way of singing and dancing. A typical show will include a bright and noisy Chinese Lion dance, perhaps followed by Malay girls performing a harvest dance. Colorfully clad Chinese girls may then entertain visitors to a lotus or sword dance, and there is sure to be an excerpt from a Chinese opera. The dancing is accompanied by clashing cymbals and rolling drums.

The Grand Palace, Bangkok. The glorious Grand Palace gives the visitor an introduction to the splendor and grandeur of Thailand's unique architectural style. The Palace is surrounded by high crenellated walls, and you enter through the huge Piman Jayasri double gate into the central compound.

THAILAND

Bangkok

Exotic, tropical, glistening with gold, and sparkling with colors, Thailand (meaning 'the land of the free'), is one of Asia's last remaining kingdoms. The country has been blessed with fertile soil and a warm tropical climate, combining to produce some of the most beautiful countryside in the world. Thailand lies halfway between India and China and is a Buddhist country with its own language, cuisine and indigenous culture. Although the Thais, especially in Bangkok, embrace modern living, it is the chaotic charm of the old style of life that will tantalize the foreign visitor. The Thais are justly celebrated for their tolerance and hospitality, and will often immediately call you by your first name. This is the only south-east Asian country not to have been colonized, and thus it has retained a unique heritage of culture and tradition which, in its remarkable harmony between nature, religion and community, is a source of inspiration to the world.

Bangkok, lying by the river of Chao Phraya, is the main commercial center of Thailand and one of the most exotic cities of the Orient. The first impression is of a city bathed in the golden rays of a deep red sun; indeed it is no suprise to know that Bangkok was called 'the city of angels' at the time of its founding. Owing to the Thais' strong sense of tradition you will find that new buildings have not always replaced old, but are built alongside, thus preserving the effect of a timeless city. Buddhism, the main Thai religion, has always been the inspiration behind the art of Thailand, and Bangkok plays host to some of the finest manifestations of this art. By far the oldest and most famous of the temples is Wat Phra Kaeo situated within the walled enclosure of the royal palace, where groups of young, shaven-headed monks beam radiant smiles at all who pass. The temple houses the beautiful Emerald Buddha, the country's most famous and precious image. It is actually made of a rare jasper. Three times a year in an auspicious ceremony, the robes of the Emerald Buddha are changed by His Majesty the King. At Wat Trimitr, the Monastery of the Golden Buddha, the ten-foot-high golden idol shines in the gloom like a radiant jewel.

The Grand Palace, a city within a city, can be entered through the Vised Chaisri Gate, and in moments you will be transported back into the days of old Siam. The Palace has opulent carved spires, gateways guarded by animal-like monsters, huge banqueting halls and quiet cloisters where saffron-robed monks sit amongst the banyan trees.

Bangkok temple dance. These traditional dances were only performed by women in the inner court of the Royal Palace, although these days roles such as the young monkey god are taken by young men. The dancers are trained from a very early age, as some of the contortions demand great flexibility. For example, the fingers sometimes have to bend back gracefully as far as the wrist. The dancers wear elaborate gold and jeweled costumes with masks and heavy make-up. Every gesture is highly stylized and a performance can last for as long as eight hours.

Golden Buddha, Bangkok *left*. The most famous of the Golden Buddhas is to be found in Wat Trimitr in a simple chapel to the left of the main temple. This Golden Buddha was found by accident when a large stucco Buddha was being moved to a temporary shelter in Wat Trimitr. The hook holding the heavy Buddha broke, and the Buddha fell, cracking open the stucco to reveal 5½ tons of solid gold. The historians believe that the Golden Buddha was covered in the stucco to hide it from the 18th-century Burmese invaders. The statue itself is thought to be about 700 years old.

A fascinating Thai pastime can be enjoyed at the Pramane ground outside the Royal Palace. If the weather is windy, the Thais will be hoisting their colorful giant kites to the heavens. The great male chula kite, with its team of handlers, is assailed by numerous female pakpao kites, which try to ensnare the male kites with their loops as they fly from one end of the grounds to the other. For the more aggressive participants, there are the kite fighting sessions.

Emerging from this preserved ancient world into the jostling bustle of Bangkok's streets can be somewhat disconcerting, but here there are also captivating discoveries to be made on every corner. Soon the visitor will stumble upon one of the city's teeming market places where the air is a confusion of smells including pungent raw spices and dried fish, and the sweet fragrance of jasmine leis. There are specialty markets such as the Nakhon Kasem market which offers an assortment of Ming porcelain, bronzeware, wood carvings and jewelry, or Phahurat market where fine silks, intricate lacework and brightly colored cotton prints can be found. A journey into Chinatown will be rewarded by shops and stalls displaying a razmatazz of wares such as birds' nests, Tiger Balm, barbecued duck, assorted teas and medicinal herbs to cure every kind of ache and pain.

The exotic blend of flavors found in Thai cuisine is due to the wide influence that India, Malaya and China have had on the indigenous palate. The restaurants are mostly owned by the Thai Chinese; they are plentiful and scattered all over the city, and many of them are open-fronted and inviting. You will find that most foods are hot in flavor, and some careful research into the chilis used will prevent a fiery mouth.

Wat Po, Bangkok *below*. The Wat Po is the oldest and largest temple in Bangkok, and covers nearly 8 hectacres. The temple is divided into living quarters for the monks and the various religious buildings. The temple was seen as a means of educating the people, so all the artifacts inside have a temporal as well as a spiritual message. One can find inscriptions relating to morality, astrology, archeology and even military defense. The primary attraction in the temple is the 150-foot-long reclining Buddha which is covered in gold leaf. It is the largest Buddha in Thailand.

Otherwise the Thai way of following fire with steamed rice should ease the tender palate. The dishes are flavored with many aromatic herbs and spices such as fresh coriander, cinnamon, garlic, nutmeg, and basil. A typical meal may start with a very refreshing lemon grass soup, followed by chunks of chicken fried in soy sauce, sesame oil and oyster sauce, all wrapped up in a leaf. This may be accompanied by a fish curry or the traditional rice and noddles with small side dishes of fried shrimp, small fried fish and mixed fruit and vegetable salad. To finish the meal one could eat any of the superb local fruit such as papaya, jackfruit, watermelon or mango, or else indulge in one of the multicolored ice creams mixed with peanuts and whole kernel corn. But don't forget, you don't have to eat in a restaurant. There are hundreds of stalls with ready-to-eat food, the exotic aromas tempting you to buy. Here you can pick up snacks on skewers to fortify yourself

Wat Phra Keo, Temple of the Emerald Buddha *above and right.* This temple is without doubt one of the world's greatest buildings. It was originally built by King Rama I in 1782 to house the Emerald Buddha, the most sacred Buddha in Thailand. The Buddha, only 30″ high and actually made of jasper, sits on a gilded altar within a blue-tiled enclosure. The deeply religious Thais prostrate themselves below this sacred image, burning incense and offering flowers. Above the Buddha is a nine-tiered umbrella, and on either side are images of the sun and moon made out of crystal.

as you make your way from temple to temple.

Many of the traditional crafts are still practiced today. Lacquer work, which can be purchased throughout Bangkok, is one of the best known. A wooden object, such as a box or a tray, is first coated with a black resin made from plants found in northern Thailand. The chosen design is then drawn on the surface and the parts which are to remain black are painted with a pigment of arsenic called 'king's yellow'. A thin coat of a different colored lacquer is then applied to the whole surface and gold leaf placed on this. Next day the piece is washed with water and the gold leaf is peeled off to reveal the black design.

Thai silk is another world-famous product. Making silk was, for a long time, an essential part of a young girl's upbringing, and many used to rear their own silk worms, make the yarn and weave clothes for all the family. Eventually, when the girls married, they would produce their *pièce de résistance* – the bridal gown.

An interesting and very different place to visit is the Pasteur Institute's snake farm, where one can see vipers, cobras, and banded kraits milked for their venom. This is the world's second largest snake farm.

The floating market, Bangkok *right*.
After the temples, the floating market of Bangkok is Thailand's most famous tourist landmark. It is the remnant of a fast waterway network which used to criss-cross Bangkok, giving the city the reputation of 'The Venice of the East'. Now there are only a few canals left. The market reaches the peak of its activity at about 7:30 am when the Klong Dan near Wat Sai is crowded with hundreds of small boats loaded down with rice, nuts, fruit, vegetables, dried fish, and rice. Lovely Thai girls in their wide-brimmed hats haggle over prices and often pose for photographs.

Another of the places worth visiting is the Rose Garden, west of Bangkok. Here you can see lush tropical gardens: the roses and orchids are world famous. Thai people can be seen working at their crafts, and for the brave, a ride on an elephant will be a most enjoyable (and certainly unforgettable) experience.

South-east of Bangkok is the world's largest crocodile farm where 20,000 crocodiles and various other reptiles are farmed. Controlled farming prevents these endangered species being hunted and from dying out completely.

The ancient capital of Thailand, called Ayutthaya, is situated north of Bangkok, on the junction of three rivers. It used to be an important trading center on the route from India to China and many fascinating ruins testify to its former glory. The principal ruins which lie around the Royal Palace are the teak pavilion, the huge Buddha at Wat Phra Sri Sarnpet and, a boat ride away, the Wat Buddhai Sawan where the founder of the city, Prince U Thong, camped while the city was being constructed. The Thais are a very warm people and the traveler will soon understand why this country is known as 'The Land of Smiles'.

Bang Pa In, near Bangkok. This is a
collection of palaces used by the
Thai kings for their summer retreat. A
pleasant way to reach Bang Pa In is
to take a pleasure boat along the
river. The buildings date from the late
nineteenth century, from the reign of
Rama V and Rama VI. The White
Palace near the lake is an intriguing
mixture of Italian and Victorian styles,
very restrained in comparison with
the superb example of Thai
architecture which appears to float
above the center of the lake. This is
the famous Aisawan Thi Paya
pavilion, probably the most
photographed building in Thailand.

Elephants and their handlers *below.*
Elephants in Thailand are hard-
working creatures. When they are not
giving rides to tourists, they are
dragging trees which have been
felled for forest clearance.

Bangrak market, Bangkok *left.*
Bangrak is one of Bangkok's busiest markets, where hundreds of stalls and barrows sell mounds of fresh fruits and vegetables of such diversity that one can only wonder at the range of Thai produce. There are bananas, fresh papayas, juicy pineapples, mangoes and the much-sought-after durians which are large, spiky, ancient-looking fruits with a strong smell. They are eaten in a salad or dipped in sugar. The market is so popular because the people of Bangkok consider that the produce is the freshest as it comes direct from the farms upriver.

The floating market near Nakhom Pathom *right.* There are many pleasant journeys to be made just outside Bangkok. The floating markets on the klongs are only an hour away from the city, yet these are rarely visited by tourists. Other enjoyable short trips are a visit to the crocodile farm, 19 miles from Bangkok, the marvels of the ancient city of Ayuthaya 50 miles away, and the famous Rose Garden on the Tachin river. These beautiful gardens also have boating, water skiing, a golf course, excellent restaurants and a Thai village which offers an exciting cultural show.

TRAVEL TIPS

The climate in Thailand is hot, so make sure you drink plenty of soft drinks, put an extra sprinkling of salt on your food in the morning, and take plenty of cotton clothes.

Bargaining is an accepted aspect of Thai life: any goods, except in a department store, are fair game for half the marked price.

It is advisable to be aware of the following customs. Never touch anyone on the head, which is considered sacred; never point your feet at a person, as the foot is thought of as the basest part of the body; and never act disrespectfully to an image of Buddha or to a royal image. When visiting temples, treat these holy places with respect by removing your shoes and not wearing any provocative clothes.

The saffron-clothed monks of Bangkok *left*. Walking through Thailand it is impossible not to notice the beaming faces of the many young monks. These monks, moving with grace and dignity, carry a saffron satchel in one hand and a brass alms bowl in the other. Usually they enter the priesthood for a period of between one and six months when they are expected to oberve the spartan way of life. This means that a monk's only possessions will be his bag, bowl and clothes. He will eat two simple meals a day and perhaps go to a school attached to a temple.

Li River, Guilin. This eerie scenery, unique in China, has inspired native poets and painters for centuries. By a geological quirk, the limestone that was once a seabed was forced upwards and then deeply dissected to create the tall fingers of rock. These have been carved by wind and rain into unusual shapes. The local people have given names to some of the strangest, such as Elephant Trunk Hill or Faded Brocade Hill. Beneath lie huge cave systems.

CHINA

Hangzhou • Peking

Shanghai • Suzhou

The Chinese civilization is over 4000 years old and is one of the most ancient in the world. Early travelers returned to their home countries with tales of the gorgeous East and laden with silk and ivory, to fire the imaginations of curious Westerners. For China is a strange country. Completely isolated from outside influences, the Chinese evolved a way of life very different from that of the West. They devised their own calligraphy, medical cures and superb cuisine. They developed a highly individualistic style of art, and it is only more recently that religious and cultural traditions from other populations have been absorbed.

Today's visitor will be fascinated by China's rich heritage. For example, a variety of splendid architecture (from the Great Wall to the exquisite Ming palaces) has survived from China's turbulent past. But man's feats are only a fraction of the whole. Nature has endowed China with great beauty, from undulating deserts to majestic mountains, from vast plains to lush bamboo forests (home of the elusive panda). The result is that the traveler is continually amazed by the diverse scenery and uplifted by the skillful creations of this ingenious people.

Mysterious and inscrutable, yet genuinely kind and friendly, the Chinese welcome tourists, but not with the neon commercialism or electronic marvels offered by other countries in the Far East. Indeed, China makes few concessions to the tourist – the street signs are in Chinese, and the food is uniquely different – and this is what makes the country so exciting and challenging to a Western visitor. It has preserved its customs and traditions for thousands of years.

China is one of the biggest countries in the world, stretching over three and a half million square miles from the Gobi Desert in the west to the Pacific Ocean in the east, and embracing a wide range of scenery. It has the largest population of any country – now around a billion – and it is the sheer number of people that strikes the first-time visitor.

Peking (Beijing) is a quiet and dignified city which, except for brief periods, has been China's capital since the beginning of the fifteenth century. Unlike many other capital cities, it has few high-rise buildings because an early emperor decreed that none should be higher than his own palace. Peking was built as a series of cities within cities, and the inner-most one, surrounded by a deep moat and a high red wall, was the Forbidden City (which included the Imperial Palace) where Chinese emperors lived for 500 years. With them were their families, concubines, priests, officials, and sometimes as many as 6000 cooks. They all lived a life of luxury in magnificent surroundings, in stark

West Lake, Hangzhou. The huge West Lake is like a Chinese willow-pattern plate that has come alive. As early as the twelfth century the area was favored as an imperial residence. The lake is one of the most beautiful in China and is surrounded by gentle wooded hills.

41

Hall of Supreme Harmony, Peking *below*. For five centuries, the Forbidden City was the residence of the Chinese emperors, who lived in complete isolation from their subjects. The Hall of Supreme Harmony is the largest of three palaces within this great city. It was used on state occasions, for celebrating the New Year or the Emperor's birthday. Rolling drums and striking bells would announce to the officials silently waiting in the spacious courtyard that the Emperor had set off for the ceremony. He was carried up the central marble ramp, (which is carved with a dragon), to his golden throne inside the lofty hall.

The Summer Palace, Peking *left*. From 1750, the Emperors of China used to go to the Summer Palace seven miles north-west of Peking, to escape the torrid summer heat of the capital. Set in an enormous park, the Palace is bounded in the south by Kunming Lake, and in the north by Longevity Hill.

Tienanmin Square, Peking *below*. This vast square, the largest in the world, is capable of holding a million people. In Chairman Mao's day it was frequently used for mass parades and processions. Every flagstone is numbered to enable the parading units to stand in the correct place. The 117-foot high obelisk is the Monument to the People's Heroes, erected in memory of those who died in the cause of the Chinese Revolution. A bas-relief shows the most important events of the Revolution, and an inscription written by Mao states 'The people's heroes are immortal'. The modern design of the buildings around the Square – one contains Mao's embalmed body – is in stark contrast to the elegant Ming style of the Forbidden City close by.

contrast to that of the people. Today's visitor approaches this 250-acre site through a series of imposing Ming palaces and pavilions, separated by huge courtyards, and linked to one another by marble bridges and endless flights of steps. Bronze lions and mighty cauldrons guard the entrances, and the curving roofs, glazed with imperial yellow tiles, glow golden in the sunshine. On each roof ridge is a row of stone dragons or other mythical beasts which were believed to drive away evil spirits. Inside the buildings are a wealth of treasures – jewelry, paintings, porcelain, embroideries and ornate furniture.

On the rare occasions when an emperor left the Forbidden City, the streets had to be cleared of people, for no ordinary person was allowed to set eyes on him. Even when he died, he was carried along a special road to the Ming Tombs, a favored hillside site which, it was said, was only inhabited by good spirits. This Sacred Way, leading to the Tombs, passes through arched gateways – the middle gate was opened for an emperor. A large stone tortoise, the symbol of longevity, marks the beginning of the tree-lined Avenue of Animals, another section of the burial route. These huge stone figures, some representing real animals, some mythical, sit or kneel at the roadside. Beyond are the Tombs themselves, behind majestic facades and enclosed by heavy marble doors. Coffins have been opened to display priceless jewels. As the greatest storehouse of Imperial China, Peking could occupy the visitor for months, with its temples and museums, palaces and parks. But the rest of the country has even more to offer.

Although Shanghai is China's largest and most sophisticated city, with a population of over 11 million, it is also the least Chinese in

The Great Wall of China *right*. This is one of the most impressive sights in the whole country. Built over 2000 years ago to deter marauding invaders, it is a marvel of engineering skill. The Wall still stretches for a distance of over 3500 miles in northern China, from the Gobi Desert in the west to the Bohai Sea on the east. The Wall closely follows the contours of the craggy hills for mile after mile, until it disappears into the distance. Understandably, after so many years, much of the Wall has fallen into disrepair, but the reconstructed sections enable the visitor to experience a great sense of history. Steep and slippery, and wide enough for five horses, the Wall is punctuated by lookout towers. It is still the largest rampart in the world, and the only man-made structure that can be seen from outer space.

Scenic waterway, Suzhou *below*. The river banks are very crowded in the early morning as the flat-bottomed fishing boats return home heavily laden after a successful night's fishing. The local women haul up the ornately woven baskets, into which the men have placed their catch, and carry them to the local market.

character. This is because, during the last century, European merchants secured trading concessions here and constructed Western-style buildings along the Bund, the famous waterfront. The city has some good department stores, and of particular interest to the visitor are cashmere sweaters, goosedown quilts, lengths of silk and brocade, and chrysanthemum tea. There are over 600 restaurants and, surprisingly, several cake shops selling Western favorites such as cream-filled pastries and lemon meringue pie. In the Museum of Art and History is an unrivalled collection of ceramics and porcelain with boldly colored glazes dating from the Tang dynasty.

Provincial towns should not be ignored. Suzhou, near Shanghai, is famous for its gardens, some dating from the 11th century. Exquisitely designed and simply laid out, they are the epitome of tranquility. Here the visitor will find pools of sculptured rocks, hillocks and tunnels, flowers and delicate foliage. In the south-west of China is the city of Kunming, called the city of Perpetual Spring, as its equable climate encourages flowers throughout the year. The surrounding mountains are dotted with temples and gardens, and the town itself is a popular meeting place for many non-Chinese people, who still wear their traditional brightly colored dress. Many old-style houses with painted wooden facades still stand, and along narrow alleys can be found some of the original tea houses where storytellers spin out Chinese legends to an audience of old men playing cards or smoking huge pipes.

In contrast to these homely provincial towns, the north-west of China is a wild region of deserts and mountains. In the Taishan Mountains is the extraordinarily beautiful high-level Lake of Heaven. It is surrounded by snowy peaks and the dense forests of dragon spruce. The alpine meadows are carpeted with scented wild flowers. Less than 50 miles

Boats on River Lanzhou, Hangzhou *below*. The ingenuity of the Chinese is no better typified than in river scenes, where the most extraordinary variety of floating vessels can be observed. They range from a few planks lashed together and propelled by an elderly outboard motor, to heavily laden barges traveling in convoy, or ancient junks with lovingly patched sails. Many goods are transported by water, often direct from the fields to the processing plants or warehouses.

Terracotta army, Xian *right*. In 1974, a local peasant near the northern town of Xian stumbled across what has turned out to be one of the world's most significant archeological finds. The fragment he found led to the discovery of an ancient army of terracotta warriors and horses. It is an eerie sight to look down upon the serried ranks of models. Buried to guard the entrance to the tomb of the Qin Emperor in 200 BC. It is estimated that there are about 6000 figures, but they have not all been excavated yet.

The figures were constructed with outstanding skill, and each soldier has individual features, hairstyle and facial expression, and carries real copper weapons – knives, spears, daggers, halberds and javelins – providing invaluable material in the study of military history.

Water carrier *left*. Up-to-date plumbing is only gradually spreading through China so, every day, millions of women have to perform their traditional task of carrying water. In both town and village, they can be seen running with mincing steps, the flexing bamboo pole skillfully balanced across their shoulders. At

away, amid barren, rocky desert, is the oasis town of Turpan, 500 feet below sea level and nicknamed 'the oven' because of the intense heat. Turpan is an exotic town, with a bustling market, mosques and camels. Unlike the surrounding deserts, the town is surprisingly fertile because of a series of underground reservoirs.

One of the greatest pleasures for a visitor to China is the food. Confucius said 'food is the first happiness', a philosophy which is still followed. Great skill, artistry and ingenuity contribute to its preparation. In the south, rice is the staple grain and there is an abundance of fresh fruit, fish and vegetables. The latter are quickly stir-fried to retain their flavor, while fish is steamed and meat is roasted. Outside some restaurants, guests may notice bamboo boxes containing live turtles, bamboo rats or snakes, which are considered delicacies. In the north of China, the staple grain is wheat, and dumplings replace rice. In Sichuan cooking chili peppers, aniseed and coriander are generously added to give a hot and spicy flavor. The famous Peking duck, served with its blanket of crispy skin, usually includes the favorite parts, which the Chinese consider to be the webbed feet and the tongue.

Food will be a significant part of your Chinese experience and, together with the spectacular sights that you will visit and the cultural heritage that you will observe, will make your trip to China one of the most stimulating and exciting that you have ever made.

TRAVEL TIPS

The Chinese get up and go to bed early, so lunch is served from about 11:30 am and dinner at 6:00 pm. Only the largest hotels serve later meals. In restaurants and hotels, you are likely to eat in a separate room, often screened off from other groups. Bars are rare.

There are two kinds of money: one, used by the Chinese, is called *renminbi*, but foreigners are given currency called Foreign Exchange Certificates (FECs) which can be used to buy goods from Friendship Stores, shops which cater specially for foreigners. All prices are fixed. If you buy an item over 100 years old, it must have a red seal attached, and you must declare it at customs, together with all your receipts for changing foreign currency into FECs.

48

each end are buckets brimming with water drawn from the local standpipe for household use, or taken directly from the canal for other purposes. It is a picturesque sight, but for the peasant it is heavy, hot and repetitive work. In some rural areas, fetching water several times a day may take many hours.

Bicycle riders, Shanghai *below*. Cars have not yet invaded the streets of China. The only ones on the road belong to government officials or to taxi drivers. Most people use solid and rather unstylish bicycles; there are over 5 million in Shanghai alone. The visitor must beware of being run down by a convoy of silent riders

who can only announce their approach by tinkling their bells. At night, bicycles carry no lights, and so present even more of a hazard. As with automobiles in the West, parking can be a problem, and a forest of glistening handlebars on the pavements is a common sight, indicating a bicycle parking area.

The Daigo Shrine, Kyoto. The shrines of the Shinto religion can be seen all over Japan. These should not be confused with the temples of the Buddhist religion. Shintoism has its roots in primitive nature worship, and the natural beauty of the wood and carvings with gods depicted as a tree, rock or bird, bear testimony to its ancient rituals. The shrines have gateways called *torii* which are made by placing two logs horizontally over two pillars to form an archway. Many non-religious functions are held at shrines, as they are a natural center for neighborhood gatherings.

JAPAN

Kyoto • Tokyo

Mysterious, romantic, electro-modern and chic; the splendor of the isles of Japan has captivated travelers for centuries. Here lies the legendary 'Xipangu' that Marco Polo described 'with palaces covered in gold'. The rich and exotic cultural traditions of Japan are set like jewels in a crown of post-war industrial expansion. You will find yourself in a country full of apparent contrasts, where the tranquility and serenity of the Buddhist shrines offer refuge from the furious pace of the Metropolis, and where the 20th century can be forgotten while visiting communities which have remained unchanged for centuries. The Japanese seem to have the ability to move easily between these extremes; on the one hand they will tolerate the rush hour crush at Shinjuko station in Tokyo, and on the other they will dedicate hours to perfecting the subtle intricacies of the celebrated tea ceremony. This, then, is the spirit of Japan, the cloak of the Samurai warrior containing the peaceful heart of the priest. Probably no other people are as concerned with their guests' welfare as the Japanese are. They will go out of their way to ensure that your visit to the land of the rising sun is a truly memorable experience.

The three thousand islands that form Japan remained fairly isolated until the Meiji government in 1868 opened its doors to the West. The islands stretch from Hokkaido in the north to Kyushu in the south, and they have been blessed with a wide variety of landscape and vegetation. In spring the countryside blossoms with peach and cherry trees. Chrysanthemums color the exquisite gardens in autumn. For those who wish to sample the rich history of the past, the 'Golden Route' from Tokyo to Kyoto offers 2000 temples and shrines and presents an unforgettable tapestry of tradition and pageant.

Tokyo is the capital of Japan. It has 27 million inhabitants and is the commercial heart of the nation. It is the best place in which to experience the way of life of contemporary Japanese people. A good place to start exploring Tokyo is the magnificent Emperor's Palace near the city center. The Palace, surrounded by a wide moat, is set in lovely gardens which make an ideal resting place in which to contemplate the city tour. At the entrance to the Palace enclosure, known as the Place of the Two Bridges, is the gateway which is opened to the public twice a year, on the Emperor's birthday and at New Year.

To the north of the East Garden is Kitanomaru Park, an extensive lawned garden containing the excellent Museum of Modern Art, and to the west is Chidorigafuchi Park, famous for the beauty of its cherry blossom trees, probably the finest in Tokyo. The famous Meiji Shrine

The Golden Pavilion of Kinkaku, Kyoto. This lies in the north-west corner of Kyoto city. It is the most famous building in Kyoto, and stands in luxurious grounds with groves, ponds and gardens. The present Pavilion is a replica built in 1955, because in 1950 the original building, dating from 1397, was burned to the ground.

lies in heavily wooded grounds. It is a building of traditional style created with the finest materials and the highest standards of craftsmanship. The shrine was built early this century to honor the Emperor Meiji and his Empress Shotoku. The main gateway is made out of 1,700-year-old cypress trees and is fronted by the equisite Iris Flower Garden. This is planted with over 100 varieties of this flower which blossoms in mid-June. Because the Meiji shrine is exalted amongst shrines of Japan, priests are often seen here in their traditional costumes blessing various events. To the north of the shrine is the glorious Treasure House, where articles associated with the Emperor and Empress are on display to the public.

The Ginza is Japan's premier shopping district, with long-established department stores and luxurious precincts. The Japanese are masters of the art of presentation, and the dazzling patterns and color with which they display their wares give an added attraction to the multitude of goods for sale. On the street Chuo-dori are smaller shops recalling old Tokyo, where dolls, fans, lacquer work and antiques are sold. Eiraido specializes in dance and Noh in fans, Shobisha in old woodblock prints, and Kuroeya in lacquered furniture. Within a few minutes walk either side of this thriving area a wide variety of traditional

Geisha with rickshaw *left*. The beautiful geisha girls are the primary users of the few remaining rickshaws in Japan. They can sometimes be seen arriving for their performances in these carriages. The mysterious geisha is in fact a highly trained entertainment girl who imparts an air of beauty and grace to many a small

gathering in Japan. She trains over many years to dance, sing, play an instrument and serve in the formal way. She will spend many hours preparing herself before she finally feels she is ready to appear in public. The geisha is held in high esteem by the Japanese, and she is extremely well paid.

Hochzeito temple, Kyoto *above*. This is a beautiful temple in the traditional style, with Japanese lanterns and prayer flags lining the entrance. The temple is constructed in wood, where most of the joints are held together only by the perfection of their design and fit. The colors have been chosen to reflect the somber

meditation of the priests. It is seen at its best when the autumn leaves swirl around the gardens. If you are lucky, you will hear the joyful chant of the priests celebrating a good harvest, and see the Japanese families in their best kimonos silently at prayer.

55

The tea ceremony *above*. The tea ceremony, or *chanoyu*, is an experience that should not be missed. The perfection of each small gesture, and the compression of time within the performance of the ritual is incredible. The Japanese see it as 'a religion of the art of life'.

Japanese fishing festival *left*. The Japanese, being an island people, are always anxious to please the gods of the sea. To make sure that their catch is plentiful, they always have a local festival to celebrate their particular local deity. A portable shrine is sometimes taken aboard. The brightly colored boats are made to look like birds or animals, and prayers are said while the fishermen are at work. The small shrine is taken out of its normal resting place and given this outing because the Japanese fishermen believe that even gods need a rest from their divine duties. Often the main boat is surrounded by hundreds of small ones.

goods can be found, including cultured pearls, ivory, silk, swords, pottery, bamboo furnishings and paper products. Japan is the world leader in manufacturing electronic goods and Tokyo is an Aladdin's cave of high-tec equipment.

The Japanese domestic culture is especially interesting. For example, the tea ceremony, *chanoyu*, is an aesthetic cult particularly for the educated classes, where it is regarded as a means of learning elegant manners and etiquette. For the Japanese the tea ceremony is 'a religion of the art of life', symbolized by the ritual preparation and serving of powdered green tea. There are many schools with different ways of conducting the ceremony, and many will be open to the public at certain times. Another aesthetic attainment of the Japanese people is the art of flower arranging, or *ikebana*, which developed from the decoration of the tea room for the ceremony.

The Japanese traditional theater consists of the Noh drama and the Kabuki drama. The Noh, dating back seven centuries, is a highly stylized, austere form of theater. The actors recite the rhythmic text whilst observing the tradition of symbolic gestures. The costumes are truly stunning and their effect is enhanced by the strange masks which the actors wear. The Kabuki drama, with its elaborate sets, unique dances and samisen music, is more popular. The plays can start in the morning and continue into the late evening, but it is not necessary to see the whole performance. Many Japanese will pop into the theater for one act to see their favorite actor. The plays are a mixture of drama, dance and music where the actor is king. Even to the Japanese the

Kabuki theater *below*. The Kabuki theater is surely one of the world's greatest dramatic forms. Japan's most popular theater, its leading exponents are treated as super stars. The Kabuki, with its exquisite sets, lovely dances and fine costumes can be performed all day long, with the audience coming and going according to their favorite scenes. The stylistic drama allows the actors to overcome the fact that the language used is archaic, because the audience can recognise the significance of gestures and movements even if they do not understand the text.

Ginza, Tokyo, at night *right*. The glamorous Ginza area of Tokyo is the world's most expensive piece of real estate, and probably some of your hard-earned cash will end up there before your visit is over. The Ginza area is the center of activity in Tokyo. At night the streets come alive with a multi-colored display of neon lights and illuminated shop windows. This is the place to go for a stroll, take in a play, visit a night club, catch a film, or sit down to a superb Japanese meal. You are quite safe to walk there at night, and if you've had a little too much *sake*, don't worry, you will not be alone.

The Rakusui Garden, Kyoto *below*. This beautiful and extensive garden in Kyoto reflects the Japanese style of gardening where formal layout, combined with natural growth, give the impression of a timeless place for meditation as well as horticultural interest. The gardens themselves are punctuated by walkways with wooden pillars and lintels flowing with climbing plants such as wisteria and jasmine. The Japanese love to place their gardens by the water, and construct beautiful wooden bridges and stepping stones to complement the waterside vegetation.

Sumo wrestling *left*. This is traditionally Japan's national sport. Sumo (pronounced s'mo) is a ceremonial, ritual type of wrestling match, where the loin-clothed wrestlers, often weighing a massive 350 pounds, struggle with each other within a sanded ring. The rules here are quite straightforward. The wrestlers start by squatting and looking daggers at each other, then, on the referee's signal, they charge and grapple. The winner of the match will be the wrestler who pushes his opponent outside the 15-foot ring, or makes him fall down within it.

Sukiyaki *right*. The art of Japanese cooking is famous throughout the world for its unique taste and wonderful visual presentation. Here we see the popular sukiyaki dish. This is served in the normal Japanese room, where the diners sit on cushions laid out around a low table. On the table sits a heavy cast-iron flat-bottomed pot, heated by a gas burner. Next to the burner is a large plate holding all the raw ingredients which are then placed in the heated pot by the waitress and cooked in front of the guests. The guests then serve themselves with chopsticks from the dish containing delicious sliced beef, tofu, vegetables and onions.

language used is archaic, but it is the style and expression in the performance that are important. Most troupes provide foreigners with synopses of the plays, and an evening at the theater will transport the visitor to a previous age of spectacle and mystery.

The Japanese not only enjoy watching sports, they are also very keen participants. Sumo is traditional Japanese wrestling, and they are also very fond of the martial arts, such as aikido, kendo, judo and karate. Baseball has become the most popular of sports, and you will see small pitches all over the country.

Japan's cuisine is the most beautifully presented in the world and is an exotic feast for Western visitors. Two famous dishes which will give the traveler a good introduction to Japanese food are tempura and sukiyaki. Tempura is seafood and vegetables lightly deep-fried in batter; sukiyaki is thinly sliced beef, various root vegetables, long onions and tofu (bean curd) cooked at the table in a shallow iron pot.

Probably the greatest Japanese dish is raw fish either in the form of sashimi or sushi. Sashimi is sliced fresh raw fish served on a long dish with radish and seaweed. For sushi the raw fish is prepared with rice flavored with vinegar. It is often eaten in special sushi bars, where all the different kinds of sushi are displayed.

TRAVEL TIPS

Given the language problem and lack of signs in English you may be forgiven for thinking that Japan is a difficult place to get around. However, the patience, honesty and courtesy of the people will help you surmount all obstacles. The golden rule if you're in trouble is to ask. Even if you are not understood, you will get a helping hand.

Japan has a mild spring (March), a warm to hot summer, wet autumn (September), and a clear but cold winter, so dress accordingly. When viewing temples or staying in inns, you will be required to remove your shoes, so a pair of slippers will be useful.

The Japanese do not approve of tipping, but small gifts for hospitality are traditional and will be treasured. The water all over Japan is quite safe to drink, and so is the food to eat, so plunge in and enjoy yourself. One last tip: in case you get lost, ask your hotel for a card with the hotel name and address on it. You can then show it to anyone for directions.

Mount Fuji, the sacred mountain. This mountain, which stands 12,388 feet high, has become synonymous with Japan, and certainly it holds a very special place in the hearts of most Japanese. It is an extinct volcano which last erupted in 1707. It can be climbed using one of six different routes with various rest points en route. For those short of breath there are jeeps to help you on your way. The brave climber may be rewarded by a spectacular sunset or sunrise over the Japanese alps, or the Pacific Ocean far in the distance. The bullet train, traveling at up to 110 mph, will speed you past Mount Fuji on the line between Tokyo and Osaka.

Index

Acknowledgements

The publishers thank the following for providing the photographs in this book:
The Photo Source/CLI 10, 24, 26–27, 30–31, 33 below, 34, 36, 43 below, 54–55, 61; Zefa 1, 2–3, 4–5, 6–7, 8–9, 11, 12–13, 13, 14–15, 15, 16–17, 18–19, 20, 21, 22, 23, 25, 28–29, 30, 32, 33 above, 34–35, 37, 38–39, 40–41, 42, 43 above, 44, 45, 46, 47, 48, 48–49, 50–51, 52–53, 54, 56, 57, 58, 58–59, 60, 60–61, 62–63.